# KEEPING IT WRITE!

---

## AN ANTHOLOGY
## WRITTEN BY YOUTH FOR YOUTH

---

by My Sister's Keeper
& Tanesha S. Windom

*Cover Design & Formatting by:*
Ya Ya Ya Creative – www.yayayacreative.com

ISBN  978-1-7356635-0-0

PRINTED AND BOUND IN THE UNITED STATES OF AMERICA

*Thank you* to the Erb Family Foundation, Community Heart, ArtOps, Youth Service America, Mott Foundation, the Corporation for National & Community Service, and Wayne Metro Community Action Agency for funding the *Keeping It Write!* project and providing platforms for art expression, youth voice, and skill development. Without you, this amazing work would not be possible. Thank you to George Washington Carver Academy, Alecia Rushing, Brenda Perryman, Tenita C. Johnson, Calvin Ray, Valicia Ward, Supa Emcee, Jonathan Wynne, Joshua Davis, James C. Turner, Sheila Finn, Nyambe Nicole, Parents, and Family and Friends of My Sister's Keeper and My Brother's Keeper who contributed to the completion of the *Keeping It Write! Anthology Written by Youth for Youth.*

# FOREWORD

by Tanesha S. Windom
*Founding President &*
*CEO of My Sister's Keeper*

First a cautionary caveat, I am a "wordy". I challenge youth to Google any unfamiliar terms contained in this preface and incorporate them into a more expansive vocabulary. I developed an affinity for writing at a very young age. The pen is empowering, therapeutic, cathartic, expressive, imaginative, and liberating. The art of writing can open doors, seize opportunities, make connections, create wealth, and curate health. Throughout my life, I have had the inherent God-given ability to tap into this power and use written words to write, and thereby, to right many wrongs. I fell in love with the nuisances of an array of verbiage, the commanding of nonverbal attention, linguistic proliferation, semantic navigation, life-changing narration, and the page-turning captivation of word utilization. I deeply wish to share my passion with the youth of My Sister's Keeper, My Brother's Keeper, and every other young keeper by design of the writing program, *Keeping It Write!*

*Keeping It Write!* is a 12-week series of writing workshops facilitated by accomplished authors, poets, playwrights, songwriters, lyricists, filmmakers, composers, arrangers, and a senior copyright attorney at the United States Library of Congress. During the 12-week installation of *Keeping It Write!* youth receive invaluable tips and instruction in writing poetry, short stories, chapter books, play and screenwriting, song and rap writing, documentary, inspirational, and biographical writing. This anthology is a collection of original works created by *Keeping It Write!* participants. It was written by youth for youth on topics relative to youth. Content covers a wide spectrum of youth-specific subjects, including self-empowerment, socio-economic status, bullying, trauma, grief, mental health, self-esteem, peer-pressure, human trafficking, gender identity issues, foster care, adoption, and life with an incarcerated parent. This amazing amalgamation of writings also features the poem, *I Decided to Keep Her*, from the My Sister's Keeper curriculum, *Keep Her: The 7 P's to Healthy Youth Development.*

I am overwhelmingly proud of this project and the gallant efforts of its contributing writers whose talent, strength, and creative prowess is evident in this manuscript. May every reader be inspired to share their stories,

successes, world views, perspectives, hurts, and hu
experiencing the literary light of *Keeping It Write*

> *"There is no greater agony than bearing a*
> *untold story inside you."*
>
> – DR. MAYA ANGELOU

Dr. Martin Luther King Jr. once said, "The time
right to do what is right." Realize the dream
*"Keeping It WRITE!!!"*

# TABLE OF CONTENTS

# POETRY

# Keeping it Write!

# TIP #1:

*"All poems do not rhyme! There are different types of poems, sonnets, haiku, villanelle, sestina, acrostic, ekphrastic, concrete, elegy, epigram, limerick, ballad, epitaph, tanka, ode, and free verse."*

– ALECIA RUSHING

# DADDY'S GIRL
## by Truth Charleston

Daddy's girl

wishing you were here

Daddy's girl

I know you're here in my heart

Daddy's girl

It's been 4 years

I'm still Daddy's girl

Can't stop the tears

Daddy's girl

I can't believe you're in jail

Daddy's girl

I still feel your pinches and imagine you're within inches

Daddy's girl

In my life there's so much tension to be

My Daddy's girl

Please come back

Sometimes I feel like I will crack

But it's a blessing that you're still alive

*Daddy's girl*

*I will survive*

*I feel like I was the one who got shot 4 times*

*I feel like I was the one who did the crimes*

*You see, I'm Daddy's girl*

*I love you so, but why did you have to go?*

*You left early in the morning while we were still sleep*

*Telling my mom you were going to work*

*Did you just lie? Did you forget your promises to keep?*

*Faking smiles, knowing the police is after you*

*We left the house just for a while,
then what did you go and do?*

*Next thing you know the police is at our door*

*Asking my mom "do you know this man?
Can you tell us more?"*

*Mom busts out crying*

*Inside I'm dying*

*Did you forget about me?*

*Remember, I'm Daddy's girl*

*The police says "he's under arrest"*

*He got shot 4 times for stealing from CVS*

*Not my Dad! Not this mess!*

*Hey hey hey, I'm Daddy's girl*

*Till this day we still all cry*

*We can't help but wonder why?*

*When I see you, will I slug you or will I hug you?*

*I think I'll love you*

*Always Daddy's Girl*

# I AM A GIRL
## by Rosa Sosa-Carroll

---

*People think I' m a  boy*

*I'm no toy*

*I am nothing to play with*

*I know I am a girl*

*I got MSK*

*I'm amazing*

*You  fools are crazy*

*Yeah maybe I*

*Might look like A boy*

*But I AM a Girl*

*I shine like a pearl*

*AND I AM GOING TO ROCK AND*

*RUN THE WORLD*

*No you are not  going*

*To  KNOCK ME DOWN*

*NOT NOW*

*NOT EVER*

*I'M GOING TO STAND MY GROUND*

*I AM A GIRL!*

# IT'S MY PARTY
by Nevaeh Elliott

---

*it's my party*

*i'll cry if i want to*

*i'm confused*

*it's my day*

*why can't i have my way*

*on my birthday, me and my family went to my granny's house to play*

*We ate cake, then in the middle of my par-tay*

*My mom started to fight with my auntie. Aye!*

*My granny said stop, "It's Nevaeh's party"*

*Then my auntie left booing*

*My dad said what were you doing?*

*My mom said nothing*

*On the fly, mom told a lie*

*I said next time no more fighting at my party*

*I don't want to cry*

*My mom said ok*

*My dad said ok*

*After all, me and my sister had a great day*

*We went to bed for the night*

*And said our prayers to sleep tight*

*My sister said god bless you*

*She said, "you know my rules about snoring"*

*I said, "I know I know I know Big Sis."*

*But it's MY party*

*And I'll snore if I want to*

# I'LL WALK WITH YOU TO THE SUN
## by Nia Nicole

*you were my light*

*in my darkest hour*

*i was your star*

*when the world got cloudy*

*always warned you*

*be careful*

*put yourself first*

*now your gone in the sky*

*and i'm left here so hurt*

*can you come back to me*

*if i pray*

*hard enough*

*i can't take you to heaven*

*but i'll walk with you to the sun*

*i love you*

*and i know you love me*

*but how could you leave me here alone*

*you were my friend*

*my brother*

*you were my one special person*

*i was your light and*

*i tried hard to fight*

*for you to change*

*and now i can't*

*is it my fault*

*or is it yours*

*honestly it doesn't even matter*

*because i just can't wait*

*for the day*

*i get to see you and hug you*

*i wanna tell you about the streets*

*and what changed*

*show you my new songs*

*and new chains*

*i dream about you all the time*

*if you know give me a sign*

*i wanna know that you listen*

*i wanna know that you're alright*

*can you come back to me*

*if i pray*

*hard enough*

*i can't take you to heaven*

*but i'll walk with you to the sun*

# I HAVE A DREAM
## by Anaya Chapman

*i have a dream*

*i know you do too*

*everybody can be equal*

*no matter if you're black, white or blue*

*i dream that the love will be restored*

*no more tears in people's eyes*

*no one will have to sit around and watch a baby cry*

*because its hungry and living in poverty*

*i'm not saying it's your fault*

*i'm not saying it's mine*

*i have a dream*

*i hope it's yours too*

*you need me and i need you*

*to make my dream come true*

*we can all stand side by side*

*no matter if we're black, white or blue*

*we can stop the hurting in the world*

*Martin Luther King and everyone's dream*
*can begin and end with you*

# MINDSET

## by Mon'a Kennedy

---

*A Mindset is a Gift from God*

*It's your intellectual thoughts*

*Your mindset is your minds promoted
thoughts Analyzed into a mental statement*

*A Mindset is your mind's perspective of life's extensions*

*It's the strongest muscle in your body*

*It plays a huge role in everyday life and
is taken for granted at times*

*Some people don't understand the weight
having a strong mindset holds*

*Having a healthy mindset is deeper than deep*

*It can give life or cause death*

*A Mindset can result in failure or breed success*

*A Mindset is a Gift*

*Don't waste it*

# IN THE MIDST
## by Carmella Butler

---

We wonder

We fear

In hope to find something more

You appear to be happy

But in reality, it's all a lie

Many nights and days

You suffer in every way

Are you happy?

Why can't I believe you right away

All the pain, you feel will never go away

But yes indeed

I am here to say

Everything is okay

You can relax now love

You are special

You are kind

You shine brighter than a fire fly

Your inner heart

*Which is so sweet*

*You can't let anybody take it for free*

*So get up and stand tall*

*When all seems like it is going to fall*

*In the midst of it, remember who you are*

*Despite what everyone else says*

*You are a star*

*Keep on being you*

*And even when you fall*

*You will say "I will rise again"*

*You are strong*

*You are powerful*

*You are beautiful*

*Everything about you is amazing*

*A true purpose indeed*

*But I need you to promise me*

*No matter how hard it gets*

*You will succeed*

*One smart cookie indeed*

*Let everyone know what you have up your sleeve*

*But of course they don't really have to see*

*You must believe*

*Believe that you can*

*Believe in yourself when no one else will*

*Because you know what that says about you*

*You are stronger than any type of herd*

*You will rise and be heard*

*So don't be afraid to learn*

*Learn new things as you go*

*As for your heart , just smile*

*And be kind*

*For it will continue to grow*

*In the midst of it be true to everything you know*

# I DECIDED TO "KEEP" HER... (with Girl Power!)

*Excerpt(s) from Keep Her: 7 P's to Healthy Youth Development, Elementary School Version*

Today, I decided Keep Her

I decided to keep her with girl power

Watch my girl magic as I become my best me

You see

I am EXTRAordinary

Beautiful, brilliant, and bright

Like a butterfly, like a ladybug

I have a special light

I decided to shine from the inside out

I decided to be Fearless and Kind

Positivity is what I am about

Poise and Posture, class and grace

On Purpose, Prepared and in Position despite the challenges I face

My Principles are my lace

Today, I gave myself the biggest hug

And I decided to Keep Her

With Girl Power!!!

## Middle School Version

*Today, I decided to keep her, Me*

*I decided that she, her, I do not want to
settle for less than my absolute best*

*I will not accept ordinary because I was born to be
EXTRAordinary*

*Mediocrity could never be good enough for me*

*It's definitive of misery*

*I decided to be the fearfully and wonderfully made*

*young woman that I was created to be*

*Greater, larger, bigger, massive, expansive, and monumental*

*Prolific, phenomenal, powerful, prominent,
profound, brilliant, and honorable*

*Notable, philosophical, deep, and spiritual yet practical*

*Elegant, sophisticated, and simple yet complex*

*Intricate, uncommon, and just as outstanding as the next*

*A light in darkness and the salt of the earth*

*I am a virtuous woman, a precious jewel, and a rare find*

*Today, I found myself*

*And I decided to Keep Her*

# FRIENDS
## by Savannah Carroll

---

*I have some pretty good friends*

*Kamiyah, Serenity, Kiona, Treasure, and Bridgett*

*They are nice and fun*

*We color, draw pictures, and laugh*

*Kamiyah is my very best friend*

*When I am sad I can talk to her*

*She understands*

*I want to make more friends*

*Sometimes its hard because some people are mean*

*But I will be my nice self*

*Friends will come*

*One day they will all want to be friends with me*

The names Helen last name Keller
Born 1880 Alabama. I was healthy chillin
In my pampers then at two years old a fever
did damage. She punished that fever left me changed
when my mom spoke to me I couldn't communi-
cate. I was blind and deaf couldn't see or
hear throwing tantrums wouldn't let anybody
near. Anne came from Boston just to be
my teacher life was frustrating I didn't
want to meet her but she, she helped me
persevere even though I couldn't see or hear

# *Write Your Own Poem*

# SHORT STORIES

# KEEPING IT WRITE!

## TIP #2:

*To develop characters in a story, play, or film, identify the goal or moral of the story. This will help to then determine the gender, race, age, physical attributes, strengths, weaknesses, and any defining personality traits of the main character and supporting characters.*

— TENITA C. JOHNSON

# THE WHITE VAN
## by Truth Charleston

One day a little girl was walking to school alone. I was walking to school too, not far behind her.  She looked kind of lonely and sad. I didn't know her, but I had seen her around. Kids bullied her and teased her, "Look at your nappy hair" "You are too dark." "You are fat and ugly." I think I saw someone push her down. I wanted to be her friend, but I didn't know what to say. I tried to catch up. All of a sudden, a white van pulled up. It stopped for like a split second. I turned my head and it pulled off. The girl was gone. I thought maybe that was her mother or father coming to give her a ride. After school that night, I was eating dinner. Mom made my favorite, meatloaf. Yum! My meatloaf fell on the floor as my mouth dropped wide open and my stomach sank. There she was all across the TV. She was on the news. They're looking for her. Where could she be? Who was in that mysterious white van? The boogie man, a kidnapper, or worse a rapist or a murderer? I told my mom, "I saw that girl and a white van." That night I had horrible nightmares about the white van. I saw it rolling up. I was breathing fast and sweating. He snatched me. He tried to touch me. I took out my body spray and squirted it in his eyes. I reached for the door. It was locked. Oh no! I was able to hit the button and escape the white van. Then, I ran and I ran as fast as I can. I screamed, "Police, Help! Help me. I lost one of my shoes. I didn't care. I reached for my cell phone. My battery was at 1%. "Please don't die! Please don't die!" I cried. I was able to call 911. The police came quick and arrested that predator. They said that he kidnapped 100s of girls and made them do things. Then I woke up. It was all a dream. Or was it???

# DREAM CATCHERS
## by Mo'na Kennedy

Once upon A time there was A young girl named Kennedy. She was African- American, and born and raised in Detroit, Michigan. As a child, she always had dreams of becoming an entrepreneur. So growing up she got into programs at school, and she joined non- profit and full-profit mentoring organizations. She had not found the type of business that she wanted to bring to the table. But one thing was for certain, she wanted her business to have a purpose. Her purpose would embody her business. So Kennedy started to explore certain talents that she was good at. She tried art, technology, counseling, and journalism. The talent that she decided to pursue eventually became her business idea, which was fashion design. This also gave her ways to input all of her talents into her business. Kennedy came to the conclusion that she would start a fashion design business or clothing line. Not only did she want a fashion business, but she wanted it to have a purpose. Kennedy started thinking of ways to help her community though her business. Kennedy always wanted to make an impact on her community. She created a name and brand name, and the brand statement for the business. Kennedy came up with the name "Klarity." The brand statement was to help center the mindsets of the next generation, to embody the success that comes out of the urban community, and give customers a taste of how we think on an everyday basis. Klarity is also all about achieving success through full- profit and non-profit business ownership. Once Kennedy had everything she needed to be successful in her business, she set goals and achieved every task on her list as the CEO of her established brand. How's that for Klarity???

# I FOUND MY DAD
## by Nevaeh Epps

One day me and my mom was watching TV. She gets an important call. She walks outside to take the call. She said she found my dad. I know my dad. Mom said no he is not your dad and she starts to cry.

# *Write Your Own Short Story*

# CHAPTER BOOKS

# Keeping it Write!
## TIP #3:

*Creating a chapter book outline of chapter titles which reflect important or interesting things about the book title; listing subtitles which include important or interesting things under each chapter title; and finally writing important or interesting things related to each subtitle will guide the writing process.*

— TANESHA S. WINDOM

# WHY I LOVE MY MOM
## by Le'Andrea Carroll

have many reasons why I love my mom. One reason is because she does everything for me, such as buy me clothes, feed me, give me transportation, and many other things. There are too many things to count how much she has done for me. I wish I could give my mom a million dollars or more, but I know that would not be nowhere near how much money she has spent on me for the last ten years. If I found a million dollars on the ground I would for sure give it to my mom. I thank my mom every day, and I tell her I love her.

My mom does lots of things and she can hardly walk, get out of her chair, and get out of the car. That is because the doctor told her she had severe arthritis. And years ago before I was born, she lived in this apartment and there was a fire. She said she was not thinking of stop, drop, and roll, and jumped out of the window. For that she got injections and it took two weeks for it to kick in. Now she is doing a lot better. I hope better things are to come to her. I hope she does NOT have to get anymore injections. I hope she gets more and more money to pay for bills in the house, our car, and TV. One of my favorite things to do with my mom is to watch TV.

*Chapter 1*
# MOM & I GO TO CHURCH

My mom and I go to church on most Sundays. My mom took me to a church convention in Indianapolis. On December 22nd, my sisters and I will perform in a play called Ornaments of Christmas. In the play, we will tell the meaning of each ornament hanging on the Christmas tree, and about the Christmas story. I will sing, act, and play the character Elizabeth. We will have a blast singing, Super Duper Christmas, Joy to the world, Come on Ring Those Bells, Angels We Have Heard on High, Go Tell It on the Mountain, and We Wish You a Merry Christmas. Elizabeth has a Merry Christmas and she can't wait to go back to school and see her teacher. Elizabeth is a lot like me. I love church, I love school, and I love, love, love my mom.

*Chapter 2*

# MOM & I MAKE DINNER

My mom taught me how to make chicken alfredo. Everybody loves it. Here's her recipe. First, we put some chicken in a pan. Then we put water in a pot with a little canola oil to boil. Add the noodles and strain when done. Cut up the chicken and add the sauce. The best part is eating it. I love learning how to cook with my mom and feeding my family just like my mom. I learn a lot from my mom. You can too!

*Chapter 3*
# MY MOM & I
# DO CHORES

hate doing chores. But doing them with my mom makes it fun. We do laundry, clean up the kitchen, clean my room, vacuum, and sweep. Mom does the mopping. My favorite chore is doing dishes because it's not too much work and sometimes I just day dream and play with the bubbles. You can turn it into a game or listen to music. My sisters help and we get the job done together. Team work makes the dream work.

*Chapter 4*

# MY MOM & I PUT UP CHRISTMAS DECORATIONS

Mom and I put up a white Christmas tree, lights, and icicles. We dressed our tree as a snow man. He has snowflakes, ornaments, a hat on top, and buttons down the middle. His carrot nose, eyes of coal, scarf, and green gloves make him look so real, especially at night. Mom lets us use our imagination and that is why I love my mom.

*Chapter 5*

# MY MOM & I
# GO SHOPPING

My mom and I go shopping at my favorite stores, Kmart and J.C. Penny's. Kmart is my favorite because they have toys. J.C. Penny has so many clothes. I like shoe stores too. All I want for Christmas is another tablet and a pink drum set. You think Mom will get it? She always gives me good gifts. That's why I love my mom so much. But that's not the only reason.

*Chapter 6*

# MOM SAYS I HAVE A PURPOSE

My mom says I have a purpose. You do too. Everybody has a purpose. Everybody has something special to do. My mom's purpose is to take care of us 8 kids. She helps me with my purpose of playing the drums. I love playing drums. I guess its like I make up my own beat. "Boom boom boom" and "bing bing bing." "Bada boom, bada bing!" I decide how it will sound.  Like life, I decide what I will be. Mom helps me to decide.

*Chapter 7*

# MOM IS POSITIVE

My mom is positive because she's helpful. One day we saw a homeless person at the gas station. My mom bought them food. They didn't appreciate it. I hated that she wasted her money. But I'm glad that I have a mom that cares. If she can stay positive when someone does something like that, I can try. My mom might be too positive. Funny…

*Chapter 8*

# MOM HAS PRINCIPLES

My mom lives the Golden Rule. She treats people the way she wants to be treated. She shows love, kindness, patience, faith, sharing, and caring. Mom believes that honesty is the best policy. One time when one of my sisters had some change that did not belong to her, my mother made her take it back where she found it. A lot of people would have kept the money. But not my mom. She is a saint.

*Chapter 9*
# MOM CHOSE ME

What's really special about my mom is that she chose me. I am thankful that my mom chose me because I could have been with someone else. She adopted me when I was a baby. Of course, I don't remember much. But I'm so glad my mom chose me.

That's why I love my mom.

## *Write Your Own Chapter Book*

# PLAY & SCREENWRITING

# Keeping it Write!

# Tip #4:

"*Writing is all about starting somewhere. Create a story that's so alive that people will think that it is real. Every story must create interest and answer the questions: Who? What? Where? When? Why?*"

– CALVIN RAY

# MY NINE YEAR OLD PROBLEMS

## by Malia Jones-Taylor

**ME AND MY BFFS ARE NINE AND TEN**

### Who?

MSK Organization

### What?

Hard problems

### Where?

At home and school

### When?

Sometimes

### Why?

Because they get bullied and they have situations at home.

## by Malia Jones-Taylor

### Who?

Myself

### What?

Intelligence

### Where?

In Highland Park

### When?

Now

### Why?

Because I wanted to write about myself

## by Kennyla Jones

### Who?

Taniya and Neveah

### What?

Friends

### Where?

Subway

### When?

Yesterday

### Why?

Because I love my friends

# PEOPLE SHOULD NOT BE ON YOUR PHONE WHILE DRIVING!!!

## IT MAKES MOMS AND DADS CRY BECAUSE PEOPLE GET HURT

### Who?

Drivers

### What?

Texting

### Where?

Car

### When?

Driving down the road

### Why?

Because it can cause an accident and people get hurt

# *Write Your Own Play or Show*

# SONG & RAP WRITING

# KEEPING IT WRITE!

## TIP #5:

*A song can be written about anything by describing associated characteristics, features, and/or experiences, such as a trip to the grocery store.*

— VALICIA WARD

*A rap may be created by using something as simple as the letters of the alphabet as a guide for your rap flow.*

— SUPA EMCEE

# SNACK BAR
## by Le'Andrea Carroll

---

I hopped into the car

I hit the snack bar

I had no gasoline

So I couldn't get far

My friends were with me

They were hungry

So we walked to the gas station

And filled our tummy's

# MY RAP
## by Rosa Sosa-Carroll

I had a BAT

Then I hit my CAT

That ate a RAT

And had on a HAT

Then he SAT

On a MAT

Next to a NAT

Named PAT

And DAT was THAT

Then he became FAT


A CAT SEEN A RAT THAT SAT ON THE
MAT. HIS NAME WAS PAT. HE HAD A HAT
AND THE BAT WAS FAT. A NAT WAS FAT
AND FELL ON THE CAT.

# MY A, B, C'S
## LIKE SUPA EMCEE
by Selena Sosa-Carroll

I'm like a star <u>A</u>thlete

I always try to do my <u>B</u>est

I am super <u>C</u>reative

<u>D</u>rawing beautiful flowers like on a girl's dress

I wish to <u>E</u>ncourage others

With my <u>F</u>avorite things

I'm <u>G</u>reat on purpose because
I love to dance and sing

<u>H</u>aving fun, I've just begun

<u>I</u>ntelligent and kind

<u>J</u>ust watch what I will do in life

<u>K</u>eeping myself and with my mind

Showing <u>L</u>ove and working hard

<u>M</u>aking good grades on my report card

<u>N</u>ever letting things get me down

<u>O</u>thers see me shine. They see my crown.

<u>P</u>ositive attitude always

I am a <u>Q</u>ueen

Carrying myself with <u>R</u>espect and Dignity

<u>S</u>haring what I've learned I'm so pretty

<u>T</u>alking, thinking, acting like a lady

I <u>U</u>nderstand it's great to be me

I got the <u>V</u>ictory

I am <u>W</u>inning

Like an <u>X</u>-ray

<u>Y</u>es, I slay

My <u>Z</u>est for life is real, and this is how I feel.

# YOU AIN'T REALLY DOWN
## by H.P. Girl

You ain't really down

If you playin' round

Class clown

Don't know the difference between
a verb & noun

You playin' yourself

When you don't do your best

Missing class

Coming in last

Yep you on blast

Didn't do the work

Ain't study for the test

Doin' too much

And doing less

Follow the rest

No educated guess

You givin' up

Not livin' up

To the standards set

To the dream Of the King

Martin Luther

Had a dream

The world awaits you

delivering

Everything that you bring

Your awesomeness

Your bossin' up-ness

The king in you

What you gone do?

A king

A queen

A VIP

Record breaking

Trail blazing

Making it pop

Always on top

Head of the class

Just like the slime

You mold & shape in your hands

Your future

Shoot ya

Best shot

Don't stop

You best believe Black girls rock

Black lives matter

Shut out the chatter

All the haters, naysayers

Everyday you slay

Til we receive equal pay

Just do it

Like Mike

Build your own business like Nike

Follow your dreams kings & queens

Cuz if you don't

You ain't really down

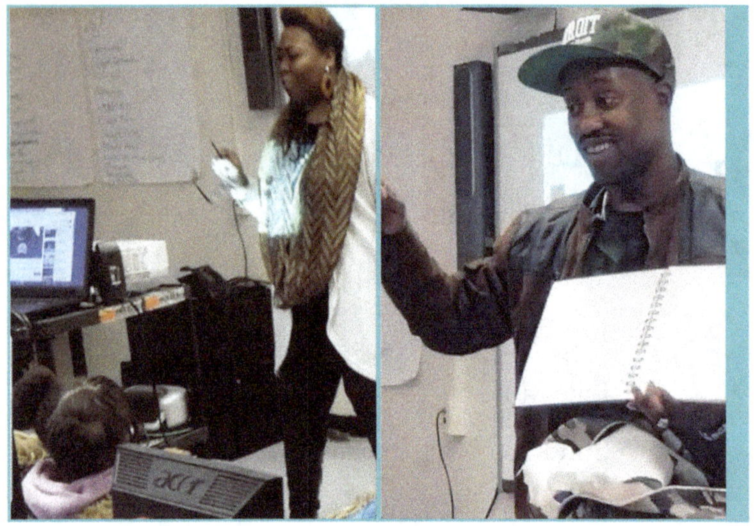

# *Write Your Own Song or Rap*

# INSPIRATIONAL WRITING

# Keeping it Write!

# TIP #6:

*Anti-thesis (what it is not), thesis (what it is), relevant question (what problem do you want to solve?), synthesis (four potential solutions to the problem), and conclusion (what can be learned?) are essential elements of any inspirational piece.*

– JONATHAN WYNNE

# 2ND GRADE PROBLEMS

by Rosa Sosa-Carroll

## Anti-thesis

Bullying hurts people so bad that they don't want to go to school

## Thesis

Going to school will be worth it in the end what will be over

## Relevant Question

How can I make it better?

## Synthesis

Do not give in, ignore them or walk away
Don't be afraid, tell a teacher, tell parents
The good will come, have a school program
Stay true to you

## Conclusion

Peace and harmony

# CRAZY HAIR DAY
## by Nevaeh Epps

I was going to school with two puff balls. Suddenly my hair popped up. Everyone started to call me Jackson Five. They thought it was funny. But I did not.

## Anti-thesis

I was having a bad hair day when my pony tails poofed and became afro puffs.

## Thesis

No hair is bad hair. I am happy with my hair and it is beautiful.

## Relevant Question

How did you learn to love your hair?

## Synthesis

Looking at myself in the mirror

Accepting myself

Finding own style

Thinking its okay to be different

## Conclusion

Nappy hair don't care. My puffy, curly, kinky hair is beautiful to me and any way I choose to wear my hair, even if it's nappy, I'm still happy. There is no crazy hair day.

# GIRL POWER
## by Kennyla Jones

### Anti-thesis

Some people think girls are weak.

### Thesis

Girls are strong because of their girl power.

### Relevant Question

How can girls tap into their girl power?

I was walking down the street. I saw my friends. A girl was sitting all alone and a boy was teasing her. I took out my cape and turned around three times. Super K came flying in to save her. We took care of the bad guys by making them invisible, laughing, having fun and living our best life. The boy sat there looking stupid. Then I turned them into big red tacos. That's me girl power.

# WHY BE SHY?
by Le'Andrea Carroll

## Topic

Shyness

## Anti-thesis

Shyness holds you back from doing what you want to do.

## Thesis

Can keep you from making bad decisions, words, and actions.

## Relevant Question

How do you overcome shyness?

## Synthesis

Let people encourage you

Face your fears

Get inspiration from others

Practice life skills, being in groups, talking in front of people, and making friends.

## Conclusion

It's OK to be shy but when it's time to shine, shine brightly

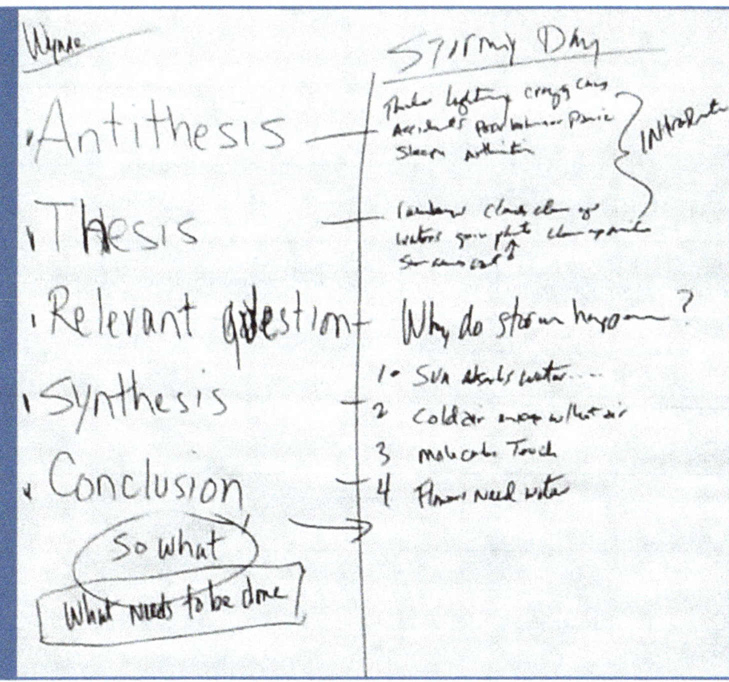

# *Write Your Own Inspirational Story*

# BIOGRAPHIES & DOCUMENTARIES

# KEEPING IT WRITE!

## TIP #7:

*Writing which chronicles and documents historical or life events generally highlights a beginning, middle, and ending.*

— JAMES C. TURNER

# MY HIGH SCHOOL EXPERIENCE

## by Mo'na Kennedy

My high school experience was partly good and bad. It's something for which I am very grateful. It has also been one of my biggest headaches. I am thankful for the opportunity. There are some things that I would change to help students develop better learning habits, and to become more productive scholars. Starting off, high school was new to me. It was different from middle and elementary school. The school was bigger, kids were bigger, and the assignments and tasks were harder. As you know high school has 4 grades. There are freshmen, sophomores, juniors and seniors. Each year was a different experience for me. Each year shaped me into who I am today. Freshman year started off scary for me. That is common for most, if not all incoming freshmen students. After I got past that stage, I got the feel of high school and started making my way through it. Getting to know peers and upper classmen was a "thing" for freshmen. Me, I got caught up being so busy with everything else but my work. It threw my grades off. With that being said, I had a rocky freshman year. As a sophomore, the year went by smoothly. I stayed on top of my work most of the year, and tried getting involved in after school activities that would keep me busy outside of school. I joined the dance team at my school. Junior year was probably my worst year of high school. I was at the age of going through that confused stage in life. School was not that interesting for me. I was just worried about passing my 11th grade year. I started off my 11th grade year shaky as well. I was worried about my grade and not the work which was impossible. I was not learning. It just frustrated me more which drove me into a skipping phase. For those who do not know, skipping is when you miss or skip class for inexcusable reasons......... WORST DECISION I EVER MADE THROUGHOUT MY HIGH SCHOOL YEARS. Why was skipping the worst decision? Well, I was missing class, which put me behind on work and knowledge. Plus, It tarnished my Record. All of these years of experience led me to my current senior year, which is full of regret, make-up work, stress, and no fun. It comes with big responsibility. Starting off as a senior for me was a nightmare. I felt like I had way too much on my shoulders and I was totally unprepared. It all catches up to you at the end. It reveals a lot of things that we seem to overlook and do not take seriously. That's why the point I am trying to get across would be, to be more focused and try grasping all information that is thrown your way, no matter how much it feels as if the teacher is not doing their job right or if their teaching skills are not working for you. There are always ways to work around it and rise above it. If you have issues within the school environment be sure to speak up and address the problem. Don't make the same mistakes. From freshman year to senior year, stay on track, step up and speak up and your high school years will be SWEET.

## *Write Your Own Biography or Documentary*

# FREE
# STYLE

# Keeping it Write!

## TIP #8:

*Free style writing does not require any set formatting, structure, or content. It simply captures what is on your mind and heart, such as a reflective journal entry or letter. It is what it is, free.*

–TANESHA S. WINDOM

# I KNOW WHAT I BRING TO THE TABLE

## by Selena Asson

*I know what I bring to the table… So trust me when I say "I'm not afraid to eat alone".*

*"Even if it makes others uncomfortable I will still love who I am".*

*I'm not the average girl from your video and I ain't built like a supermodel but I learned to love myself unconditionally because I am a queen.*

# HOW IT HAPPENED
by Anonymous

I'll never forget the day, April 24, 2015 to be exact. I was 9 years old and only in third grade. The little one was only three years old. I had just came home from school. Mom was in tears cooking dinner. It was only 4:00pm. I knew it was too early for food. Mom had put all of our clothes in trash bags. Then they were at the door. They took us away. We barely had a chance to say goodbye. That's how I got into foster care.

My advice to the younger ones in the system is to always to remember that no matter how bad things may be, it could be much worse. Keep your head up, and remember that you are here for a purpose.

# HER

## by Anonymous

---

*She's a part of every girl.*

*She's your other half.*

*She's your anger, sadness, your depression,*
*your anxiety, your fear, and even your period.*

*She's the reason you worry and have other deep emotions.*

*She's best described as Her.*
*Over the years, you've tried to give Her a name,*
*Alice, Sidney, or Destiny. But her name is Her name.*

*All women have Her.*

*You've tried to cut off Her, but she's a part of you.*

*Her makes you do crazy things. You can't tell*
*anyone about Her because they'll think you're crazy.*

*You can't tell a woman either because even though*
*they know who Her is, they've forgotten Her over the years.*

*Now you know who Her is.*
*You know what she does.*

*Don't forget Her.*

# DEAR GIRLS
## by Toni Hamm

*Dear girls,*

*Life for us is different.*
*We are judged on how we look,*
*what we wear and even our hair.*

*Boys look at our curves.*

*And we leave them shook.*

*But no one ever takes a good look.*

*At what we have inside.*

*Because on the outside looking in.*

*Everything has a good look.*

*But what's inside?*

*The things we hide inside?*

*The good traits we're scared to share?*

*Because we've been hurt?*

*Because we've been told we can't let these traits show?*

*What is it?*

*Why won't they just let us glow?*

*They say they love our inner beauty.*

*But we can never show them our inner soul.*

*They'll take control and have us feeling low.*

*But when they do make us feel low.*

*Remember this poem.*

*Remember that your inner beauty
is something they can't take.*

*We all have it.*

*We can't fake it.*

*Love your inner beauty.*

*Know that no one can take it from you.*

*Know that there's only one you.*

*And only you can be beautiful you.*

# *Write Your Own Free Style Story*

# PRAISE FOR STUDENTS

*"This published work documents the extraordinary talent and creative genius of our scholars at George Washington Carver Academy. I could not be more proud of this tremendous accomplishment which will inspire youth around the world."*

– SUPERINTENDENT SYLVIA BROWN
*George Washington Carver Academy*

*"Outstanding work!!! The courage and depth of writing revealed within this collection of writings is awe-inspiring. Tanesha has been organizing youth to showcase their talent since childhood. She has done it again with this collection"*

– CHARLENE TURNER JOHNSON
*Board Chair of My Sister's Keeper*

*"Yes!!! I am my brother's keeper and my sister's keeper. This anthology is a "keeper" and these young authors are undoubtedly Keeping It Write!"*

– FORMER HIGHLAND PARK MAYOR DEANDRE WINDOM
*Chairman of My Brother's Keeper*

*"My heart is overfilled with joy, happiness and pride for these young leaders who have pressed forward to share their stories! Big kudos and congrats to you! This is just the beginning of a great journey and your best is yet to come!"*

– TENITA C. JOHNSON
*So It Is Written Editing & Writing Services*

*"Congratulations on the release of Keeping It Write, the first of many great literary works. It was my honor to share my perspective on writing with these powerful, young storytellers."*

– JONATHAN WYNNE, M.A., M.B.A., M.ED.

*"It was an absolute pleasure meeting and sharing knowledge with the students in the My Sister's Keeper class. The youth were brilliant and told compelling stories that made me proud to be a part of this project."*

– JAMES C. TURNER
*Filmmaker, Highland Park 100 Year Documentary*

*"This is absolutely brilliant! My Sisters Keeper has taken the time and patience to develop these young writers who contributed beautifully to this anthology, and it shows. Bravo MSK!!!"*

– VALICIA WARD
*Author, Poet, Actor, and Songwriter*

*"Great job on your first of many published literary works! Keeping It Write is a youthful and heartfelt work of art. Our youth have undeniably taken a deep dig within the recesses of their experiences to create this remarkable collection."*

– JAYLEN S. JOHNSON, ESQ
*Senior Copyright Attorney, U.S. Library of Congress*

*"It takes courage, compassion, and conviction to become a writer. The youth at George Washington Carver Academy and My Sister's Keeper have presented their writings in a way that exhibits these character strengths in this anthology."*

– MARGUERITE LAWRENCE
*Vice-President, My Sister's Keeper*

# ABOUT MY SISTER'S KEEPER

Since its inception in January 2013, *My Sister's Keeper* (MSK) has positively impacted the lives of countless under-privileged and under-served youth ages 7-24. MSK has forged partnerships with area schools, churches, businesses, organizations and individuals to provide two core pathways for youth mentoring activities: Community-Based Mentoring and School-Based Mentoring. These activities include: one-on-one mentoring, group mentoring, peer-to-peer mentoring, e-mentoring, academic enrichment, life skills training, field trips, afterschool programs, community service projects, career exploration, internships, summer employment, six-week summer programming, life-coaching, counseling services.

To keep youth on the path to success, mentoring best practices are used along with evidence-based curriculums, including *Botvin Life Skills Training, The 40-Developmental Assets, and I Am A Keeper and Keep Her: The 7 P's of Healthy*

*Youth Development.* MSK mentees receive instruction in developmental topics, such as Self-Esteem Building, Self-Efficacy, Etiquette, Decision-Making, Goal Setting Coping with Stress, Controlling Anger, Emotional Intelligence, Conflict Resolution, Anti-Bullying, Social Skills, Communication Skills, Assertiveness, Peer Pressure, Entrepreneurship, Financial Literacy, Seven Habits of Highly Effective Teens, Test Taking Skills, SAT Prep, College Prep, Relationship Building, Substance Abuse Prevention, and Self-Care. This program content has been covered during the school day on the campuses of George Washington Carver Academy and Highland Park Renaissance Academy, two Title-1 K through 8 schools in Highland Park, Michigan. MSK has also offered out-of-school programs inclusive of *Sewing for Success, Chess for Success, Girls Who Code,* and the *KEEPING IT WRITE!* writing, reading, and coding after school program, which is celebrated throughout each page and every line of this published work, *Keeping It Write! Anthology Written by Youth for Youth.* For more information about My Sister's Keeper, visit our website: www.mysisterskeeeeperhp.org or contact us via email: info@mysisterkeeperhp.org.